My Father

Lee Davis

By
Bettye Davis

Copyright © 2022 by Bettye Davis. All rights reserved including reproduction in whole or in part in any form except by newspaper or magazine reviewers who wish to quote brief passages in connection with a review. No other part of this publication may be reproduced, stored in retrieval system or transmitted in any other form by means electronic, mechanical, photocopying, recording or otherwise without the expressed written permission of the author or Sula Too Publishing.

ISBN: 978-1-7365717-5-0 paperback
2022 - Sula Too Publishing

Printed in the United States of America
March, 2022

Sula Too Publishing
www.sulatoo.com/publishing

Lee Davis' Motto:

"It's not how you look, but how you feel."

He wanted everyone to be
in the best of health and to stay healthy.

*This book is dedicated to
my daughter, Lisa
my son, Christopher
and my grandchildren,
Doneria, Stephenie, Torik, and Jai'
May they share the pride I feel
as I recall a few of the key events
in my father's life.*

Bettye Davis

About the Author

Bettye Davis is the daughter of the late Lee and Ethel Davis. Bettye grew up in Tampa and attended schools in Hillsborough County. She also attended Hampton University, Bethune Cookman College and Ft. Lauderdale College and studied Business Administration.

She later attended the University of Tampa where she was trained in Medical Technology. She worked at University Community Hospital as a medical technician for a number of years.

Following her father's death, Bettye took over Lee Davis Enterprises. She served as vice president of the Tampa Branch of the NAACP for eight years.

She is also listed in Who's Who Among Black Americans. Bettye Davis has traveled throughout the United States. Her sojourn abroad includes Paris, Rome and several Caribbean countries.

Bettye offers this book as her contribution towards perserving the legacy of her hero, father, and a national treasure.

Bettye Davis

Acknowledgements

I wish to express thanks to all the people in Tampa who cared for my father during the last days of his life.

Special thanks to Mrs. Chloe Coney for she support of my father's legacy and the need for this manuscript.

My sincere thanks to Senator James T. Hargrett, Jr. for the leadership he provided in getting the beautiful Lee Davis Center established in Tampa, Florida at 22nd Street and 26th Avenue. This center, named in my father's honor, is truly a monument to the unselfish work he did in this community. Senator Hargrett's efforts, combined with those of numerous others, can be credited with keeping my father's dreams alive. His dream was to have a facility and other resources to address the health and social service needs of deserving people in our community.

Because Lee Davis was in the public's eye, many people touched his life, just as he touched theirs. Therefore, it is impossible for me to name his many friends and associates in this publication. So, whatever your role may have been in his lifetime or whatever role you may assume in the future to promote his dream, just know that you are appreciated.

Finally, I would like to acknowledge the assistance of my friend and former English teacher, Betty P. Brown Wiggins, for her eagerness and selfless help in compiling the first version of this publication and Ersula K Odom for the current version. In both cases, their generosity of spirit, resources and encouragement helped to sustain me through some challenging times and to see the project through to completion.

I love each of you for keeping alive the name and deeds of a great man - a great humanitarian -- my father, Lee Davis.

Bettye Davis

Part One

How I Remember My Father

"It's Not How You Look, But How You Feel"

Early photo of Lee Davis at approximately 25 years of age.

Lee Davis, the youngest of three children, was born April 15, 1894 to Mr. and Mrs. Primus Davis. The family moved to Tampa from Live Oak, Florida about 1912. He was born when Klan lynchings and Uncle Tomism were common. I heard first hand my grandmother (Angeline) and grandfather, recall their days as enslaved people. Their survival was remarkable.

He attended the local public schools, but stopped to get a job. He started a Pressing Club (now known as dry cleaning) as his first business venture in 1921 in Tampa, Florida.

In 1926, Lee met a beautiful lady, Ethel Small. They fell in love and was married on April 15, 1926, his birthday.

Davis Manufacturing Company was started sometime during the late 20s or early 30s in Florencevilla, near Winter Haven, Florida. Florencevilla was a black owned area somewhat like Central Avenue in Tampa. His company produced hair products for men. The company also made Lady Davis Products, including perfumes and cosmetics. He actually made these products at the family's Potter Street home. This was the beginning of the hard road to success.

Also at this time, in the early 20s and 30s, he had a race problem because of his

1920s & 30s

color. My father had a very light complexion. At times it was like being in two worlds, black and white. I heard the story about what my father and mother had to do when traveling home from their business in Florencevilla, Florida. At night on the way back to Tampa, Ku Klux Klansmen were usually on the road near Bartow, Florida. My mother would hide under a cover in the back seat of the car, because she was a pretty dark brown skinned woman. The Klansmen would routinely stop the car, look in and then tell my father to go on his way. With his heart in his hands, he would keep going.

In the 1930s, Central Avenue in Tampa was the place to be if you were black. Most of Tampa's black business establishments were located on Central Avenue. Black people owned businesses including hotels, bars, clubs and restaurants. They had many meetings, dinners, parties, parades, and dances.

My father was industrious and had a good business in Florencevilla and was well prepared to open additional businesses on Central Avenue. He opened Lee's Bar and Lee's Poolroom. The work was hard and the hours were long, but he and my mother were able to keep up with the new businesses and still maintain the business in Florencevilla.

Being the man my father was, he was always coming up with something new. He came up with a new hair product for black men. The name was No Kink Hair Cream Wave Down Hair Pomade.

1940s & 50s

Lee Davis in the 1940's

Time was moving on, but not Tampa's black community. Housing was poor or I will say very bad. My father helped save people's homes, or provided housing, clothing, food and even financial help for some. His generosity was well known, but most of the help he provided to people was without public knowledge or fanfare.

He saw and was acutely aware of the needs of his people. The status of black people's health was bad. High blood pressure, cancer, heart diseases and sexually transmitted diseases were prevalent. Mothers-to-be, babies and children needed health care.

Since most people could not get downtown to the Health De-

1950s & 60s

partment which was located on Tampa Street, my father decided to do something about it. On July 12, 1951, he and my mother gave Hillsborough County the land they owned across from their home on Potter Street and 28th Avenue for the sum of $1.00. The gift became the site where the first Lee Davis Clinic was built. His motto was, "It's Not How You Look, But How You Feel." True to his motto, he wanted everyone to be in the best of health and to stay healthy.

In the 1950s he had worked hard and aquired a great deal of land and some money. Central Avenue was going down. He built a small shopping center on 22nd Street (3515 - 3529). The complex included the Bird of Paradise Bar, Lee's Diner, College Hill 5 & 10 Cents Store, a pool room, a grocery store, and a gas station at 22nd Street and 26th Avenue. He was now president and founder of Lee Davis Enterprises.

In 1960, my father built my mother a new home. Since the home on

1960s to 1980s

Potter and 28th Avenue had been built in 1926, he felt it was time to move. Osborne Avenue was the perfect place for our big, brand new, pink house with a swimming pool.

Now that my father had worked hard all of his life and had his new home, it was time to do some of the things he liked to do. He had a great love for the outdoors. He went hunting in Wyoming and killed a black bear that became our bear rug.

He took me hunting and fishing in Thomasville, Georgia. Although I was a girl, my father took me with him because I was a "Daddy's Girl." He also took Carl and Robert who were like the sons my father did not have. Carl and Robert were adults. I was the only child on the trip.

Although my father worked hard, he always had time for his family. We went to football and baseball games together. Each summer, we traveled by car over almost all of the United States. We would be on the road for two or three weeks.

My parents were active and participating members of St. Paul African Methodist Episcopal Church in Tampa. The church honored them by hanging a portrait of them in the basement, the center of a great deal of church activity. They were generous in their donations and support of the church. Among their contributions to the church was having the church sanctuary carpeted.

My father also donated the first school bus to Middleton Senior High School. A photo once featured in "Pictures of the Past" in the Florida Sentinel Bulletin newspaper showed a picture of the bus. Over the years, the Sentinel also has generously documented my father's many positive community enrichment activities.

In 1963, one of Tampa's daily newspapers speculated that he was one of the 35 black millionaires in the United States. My father said "No." He did not want that to get out. He wanted to be known as a humanitarian.

In the late 1960s and early 1970s, since my father was getting old and Central Avenue had been obliterated by urban renewal, he sold his bar on 22nd Street.

In 1974, his health was going downhill. In fact, that year both my father and mother were diagnosed as having cancer. Both were in the hospital at the same time. From 1974 to 1981, he was at home with his family. Many days he would talk about the past and would tell me about how hard life was. He told me to always help someone if I could, because one day "You may need help." In his time, my father was the bridge builder. My father was the humanitarian. My father was Lee Davis.

I remember that January 20, 1981 was a cold, rainy day, when my mother was ill and at home with nurses around the clock, my father was also in the hospital. I was at his bedside around three o'clock in the afternoon when he told me that he was tired. He said he loved us very much and asked us to keep the family together. Then like a flash of lightning, God sent his angel down to Tampa for my father. He said, Lee Davis, come home; your work is done. For you have helped many and touched the hearts and lives of many in your life span of 87 years. The work you have done will speak for you. He was gone.

My mother survived my father by four years and ten days. She passed away on January 30, 1985.

To My Best Friend

by Bettye Davis

My Best Friend is Gone

Best friend is gone!
Oh how I miss you!

Best Friend is gone!
Not here for me to talk too,
To touch!

Best friend is gone!
Not here for me to laugh with!

Best Friend is gone!
Not here for me to walk with!

Best Friend is gone!
Not here for me, to cry with!

Best friend is gone!
Not here to go fishing!

Best friend is gone!
Not here for the hot summer day!

Best friend gone!
Not here to see fall gone and go!

Best Friend gone!
Not here to see the spring come,
To hear the birds sing

Best friend gone!
Not here anymore, what a difference
The word is going to be!

Best friend gone!
Not here anymore!

How can I go on!

Part Two
Recognitions, Affiliations, Awards & Associations

Davis donated the land to the City of Tampa for the Lee Davis Health Clinic.

President of Lee Davis Enterprises.

Chairman of Hotel Pyramid Corporation, Frontiers of America.

Chairman of Tampa Negro Businessmen League.

Second Vice-president of Washington Shores Federal Savings and Loan Association, the first black bank in Orlando, Florida. Co-founded with Ruye Hamilton Sr.

Board of Trustee member for Bethune Cookman College.

Selective Service Board Member #32 Edward Waters College.

Tampa Urban League.

Greater Tampa Chamber of Commerce

Chairman, Community Chest Fund

Mason, Elk Achievement Award - President Nixon
Lee Davis Week - Hillsborough Community College

1951 - The officers and members of Gamma Eta Sigma., Chapter of Phi Beta Sigma Fraternity, Inc., on the occasion of its Bigger and Better Business Week Observance, awarded to Lee Davis on April 8, 1951.

Citation for outstanding service from faculty and members of the Harlem School PTA for his outstanding services in the field of Business.

1961 - Certificate of award to Lee Davis from the Democratic Voters League on November 12, 1961 in Tampa, FL.

1963 - Certificate of Life Membership to Lee Davis as a Life Member of the National Association for the Advancement of Colored People on April, 1963.

1967 - The President of the United States of America awards this certification of appreciation to Lee Davis in grateful recognition of valuable service in the administration of military Selective Service Act of 1967.

1970 - Certification of Appreciation awarded to Lee Davis for outstanding service and dedicated service at St. Paul AME Church.

1971 - Champion of Higher Independent Education in Florida 1971-72.

1972 - Outstanding contribution in higher education in the interest of Negro youth was presented by The United Negro College Fund on October 3, 1972. Presented by the presidents of the Independent Colleges and Universities of Florida.

1971 - Distinguished Service Goodwill Courage and Unselfish Devotion to Others, presented by Frontiers of Arrerica, Inc., Tampa, FL, 1971.

1976 - Proclamation from the City of Tampa from Mayor William F. Poe. Proclaimed the week of November 21 through November 27, 1976 as "Lee Davis Week."

Listed in Who's Who Among Black Americans in 1977-78.

Non-partisan Registration Committee of Hillsborough County, Florida presented an award to Lee Davis for his distinguished services in the field of political action.

The United Negro College Fund presented the Award in Recognition of: Meritorious service in support of higher education for Negro Youth Chapter of Bethune Cookman College.

Hillsborough Community College student government awards Lee Davis for Outstanding Contributions For Higher Education and Economic and Social Development for Minorities.

The Bethune-Cookman College National Alumni Association presented The Shafts of Light award to Lee Davis.

"Citizen of the Week" - WTMP Radio Station.

Part Three
Photo Highlights:
A Closer Look at Lee Davis

My Father - Lee Davis

Father's first business was opened in 1926 in Florencevilla, the black business section of Winter Haven, Florida. In Tampa, based on the number of black businesses opening in the area, Central Avenue was the place to be. Therefore, Mr. Davis and my mother decided that they would open a bar and a pool room. Uncle Moses (father's brother) ran the pool room.

Mr. Davis and my mother had a bar and a little restaurant. When I was a little girl, they took me with them. I sat in the restaurant part where I could look out window and see Mr. Kid Mason down the street with his little shorts on. I remember his shorts because that is all he seemed to wear. Due to his polularity and the parties he sponsored with young people, a community center was named for him.

Lee Davis's brother Moses Lee (right) operated Lee Davis' Pool Room and Bar on Central Avenue in the 1930s

When I started attending nearby St. Peter Claver Catholic School, I walked there from Central Avenue, I often stopped at Kid Mason's for a soda or get some potato chips. Then I went by Dad's restaurant and waited for him to carry me home.

My earliest memory of Central Avenue engaged all the senses. I can still hear the sounds of people walking on the sidewalk's wooden boards going click, click, click. All the noise! I saw off-duty soldiers from McDill and people on motorcycles.

With McDill Military Base being in South Tampa, black soldiers came to Central Avenue because it was the hot spot for black people. It was the center of black business, social life, shopping, the movies and other forms of entertainment. The Lincoln Theater was one of two theaters where black people saw the latest movies. My mother and father took me to the Lincoln to see my first movie ever, The Ten Commandments.

I can still see and hear those motorcycles traveling through Central, louder than belief for the small child that I was. They frightened me and I would get down in the car to shield myself from them. Mother would say, "Well, why are you hiding from those motorcycles?" I said , " Momma, they are making so much noise. I'm scared of those things. I'm scared of those things!" Reality is the cyclists could not have been nicer people and they brought a lot of joy to the area and businesses. I don't remember anyone getting shot or killed. I do remember people moving in and out of the Central Avenue area by a cab company operating from a "cab stand."

My Father - Lee Davis

The Pyramid Hotel was a product of the Pyramid Hotel and Investment Company where my father was president and R. R. Williams, a black doctor, vice-president, Mr. Mason as second vice president, Johnnie Curtis as secretary, and Mr. E. E. Barton was treasurer. Some of the Executive Board members were Mrs. Gardner, Mrs. Rogers, Mrs. F. B. Stone, Mrs. L. B. Young, Mr. Allen Jones, Dr. Sowers, and Dr. Lewis.

The Pyramid Hotel Investment started in the early thirties. The Pyramid Hotel was one of the first black hotels in Tampa and was located on Central Avenue. Besides being a hotel, the Pyramid was popular because that's where dances were held.

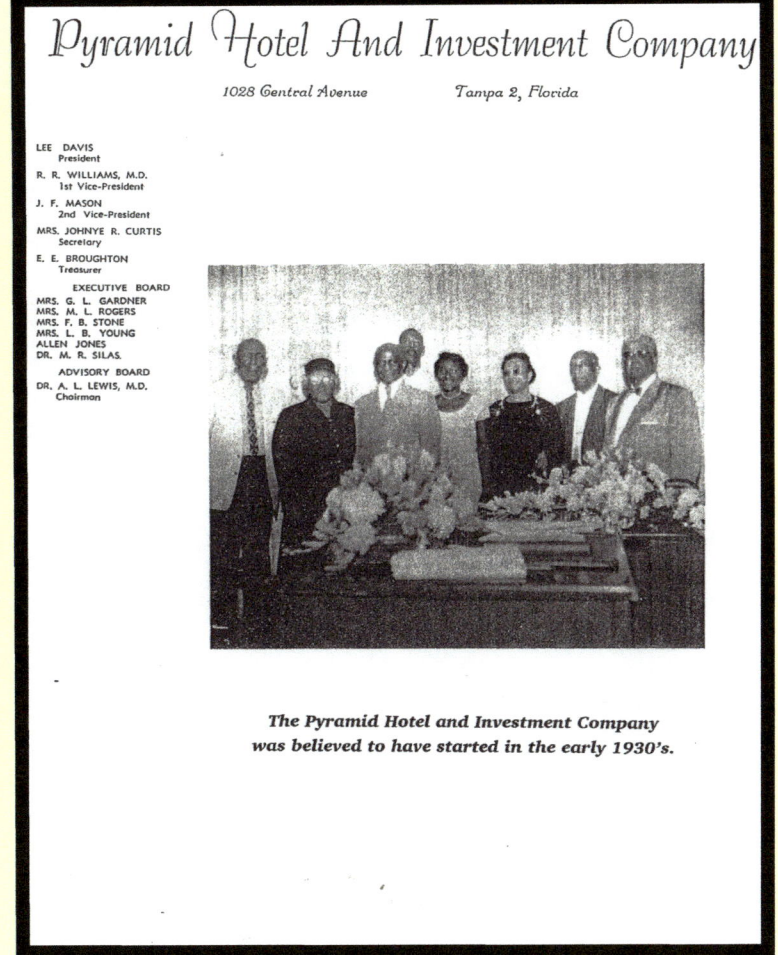

The Pyramid Hotel and Investment Company was believed to have started in the early 1930's.

The Pyramid Hotel was one of the first black hotels in Tampa, Florida.

Inside the lounge of The Pyramid Hotel

Pyramid Hotel Building in the 1950's
(Courtesy of HCPL)

Central Avenue - Pyramid Lounge. Lee Davis was president of the Pyramid Hotel

My Father - Lee Davis

Don Thompson Vocational School in Tampa with several members of the staff standing out front (L-R Lee Davis, Georgette Gardner, G.D. Rogers, Sr., Mr. Bosbo, unidentified woman, and George Carr) with a bus used for "free health checks."

Photo credit: Courtesy of the Special Collections Department, University of South Florida. Digitization provided by the USF Libraries Digitization Center.

Jeep owned by Lee Davis (driver and announcer) for the Health Test Program.

Free Health Clinic on Central Avenue in the same strip as Watts Sanderson's Blue Room

Don Thompson Vocational School in Tampa was primarily established for African American men returning from military service. The school offered day and night vocational classes such as black smithing, tailing, auto mechanics, and electroplating. It closed in 1956 and Howard W. Blake High School was opened honoring Mr Blake as an African American educator. It was under Mr. Blake's tenure as principal that Booker T. Washington Junior High School became the first accredited junior high school for African American students in Tampa.

1947 Tampa Progressive Voters League at Rogers Hotel
Standing: William Hammond, second from the right; Seated: First from the right, Lee Davis (Courtesy of HCPL)

1948 Democratic Voters League at Rogers Hotel
Standing: Perry Harvey, Sr., second from the right; Seated: Lee Davis, second from the left (Courtesy of HCPL)

Lee Davis was the parade marshall in the 1952 Tilt to the Maroon and Gold parade. I rode in the car with my dad and had the best seat in the house to people watch.

(Bettye is shown watching the parade from the back seat)

Part Four:
Lee Davis & His Productive Life

Davis Manufacturing Company

```
FRITZSCHE BROTHERS, INC.
ESSENTIAL OILS & CHEMICAL PREPARATIONS
PORT AUTHORITY COMMERCE BUILDING
76 NINTH AVENUE AT 15TH STREET
NEW YORK
P.O. Box 9 Station O

Cable Address
FRITZBRO
NEW YORK
Telephone
WATKINS
9-4100

Address all Communications to the Company

EL(MR)                                October 21, 1938

Davis Mfg. Company
Box 1826
Tampa, Fla.

Gentlemen:

          On August 8 a sample of our
    COMPOUND OIL BOUQUET #06183
was sent to you for experimentation.

     Realizing that you may not have had sufficient time
to conduct the necessary tests, we do not wish to hasten
you in your decision. Nevertheless, we are always interested
to learn how our products work out in practical processes and
whether they meet with requirements. In this respect, we
believe our services can be of valuable assistance to you.

     It is our desire to help you make a satisfactory
selection of perfume materials and at this writing we should
like to assure you of our willingness to cooperate with you
further in working out your problem and shall welcome your
comment.

                              Very truly yours,

                              C. F. Booth
                              FRITZSCHE BROTHERS, INC.
```

Lee Davis' Manufacturing Company produced one of the first hair pomade, No Kink Hair Pomade. Now it's known as "Do Hair Pomade". He had the original formula for the "No Kink Hair Pomade" that men used for their hair. It laid the hair down. I still have a copy of the patent document for No Kink Hair Pomade. He sold it to what became Duke's Hair Pomade. His picture was on the original can.

The letter shown here connects Davis now to 260-year history of essential oils. Tracking this history through time and sales, mergers and acquisitions leads us to present-day companies Dodge & Olcott and Givaudan.

My Father - Lee Davis

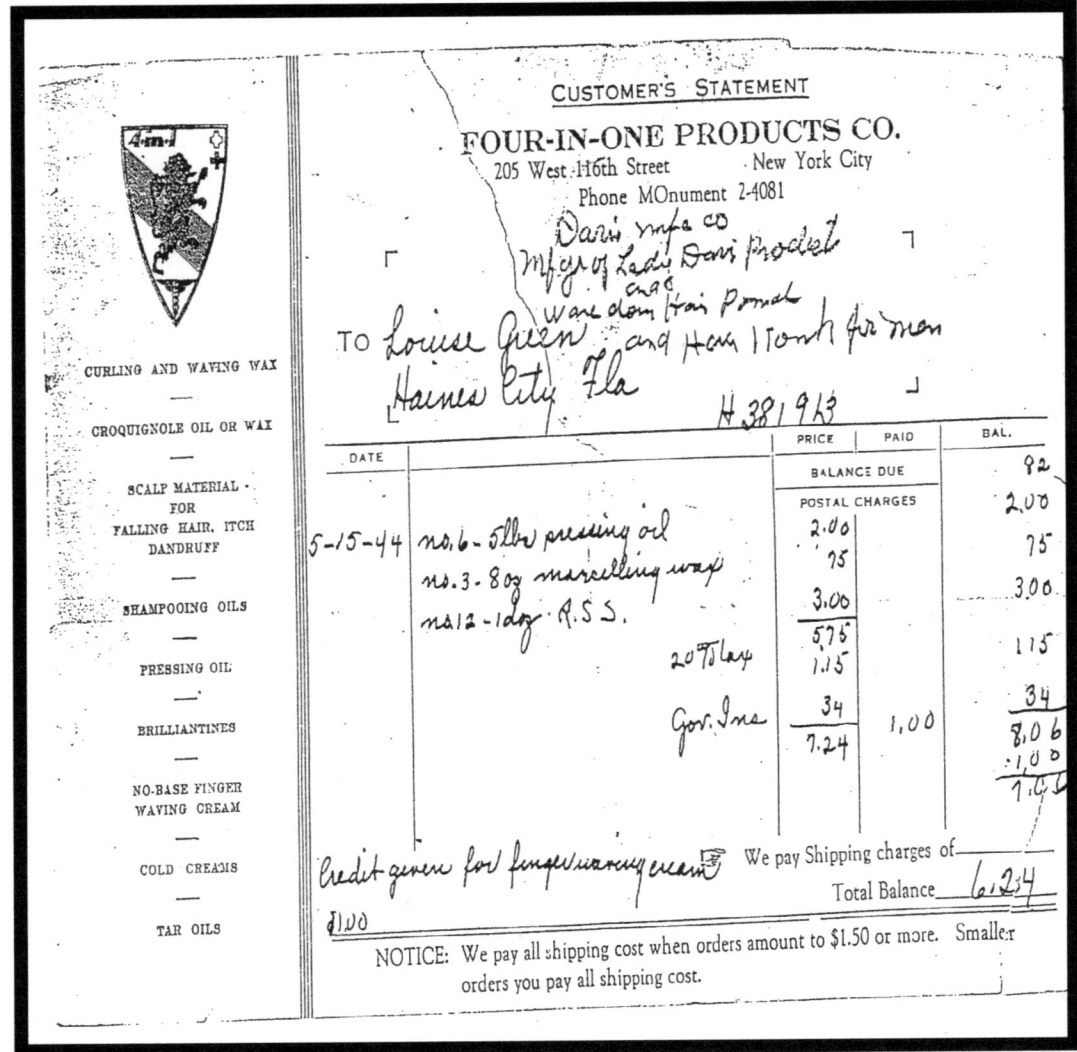

Customer's Statement
Davis Manufacturing Company
Manufacturer of Lady Davis Products

To: Louise Green
Haines City Florida

East Tampa's 22nd Avenue and West Tampa's Main Street benefited from the business migration resulting from the decline of Central Avenue.

My father owned most of the businesses in that area of 22nd Street. He owned Lee's Diner which I believed was one of the oldest remaining black restaurants since Mrs. Ozepher Harris' had closed. He rented space to Mr. Shelly Brene for his restaurant on the end of the block. He owned a BP gas station which he later rented to Mr. Buster Mitchell, operating as "Busters." In the seventies, father acquired the West Gardens on the end. Then there was the Guard and College Hill Pharmacy. There was a little man with a Bar-B-Que stand on the corner.

Central just died away and everything moved to 22nd Street and West Tampa's Main Street. Mr. White moved his Cozy Corner to Main Street. Mr. Bexely had a business on Main Street as well.

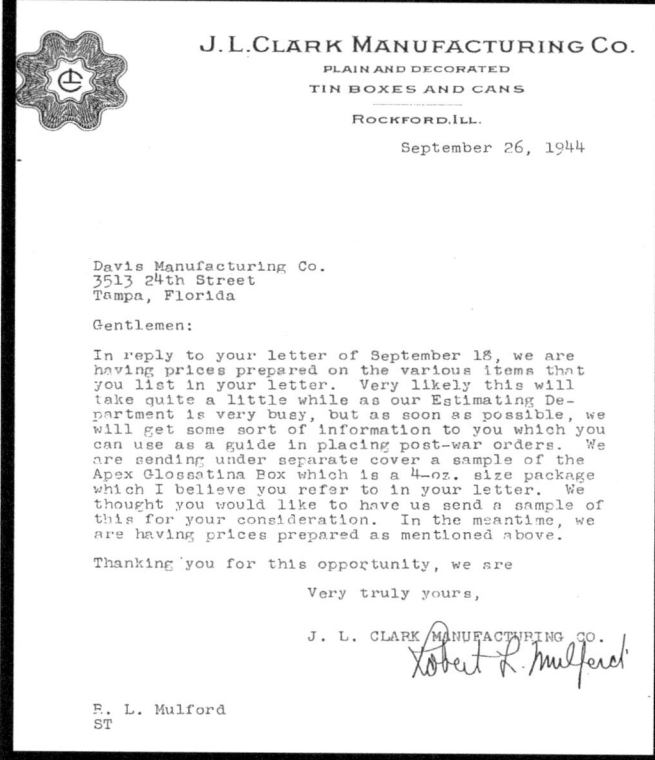
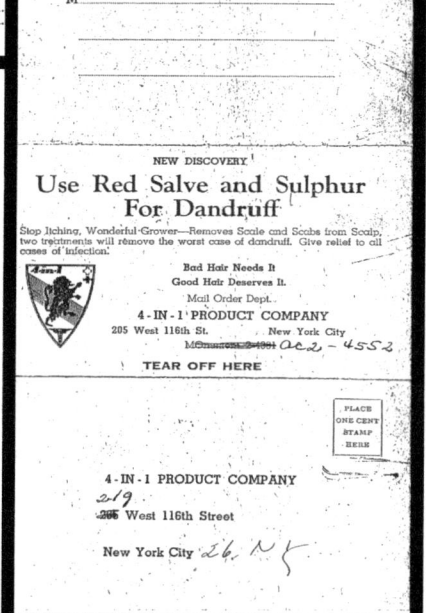

Central Avenue changed significantly when all the black businesses scattered. My father was lucky and well positioned enough to start a businesses when others could not. Starting black businesses was necessary due to segregation. He thrived on Central and then he moved his businesses from Central Avenue to 22nd Street. Unlike Davis, many people were not able to keep their businesses going.

Paradise Bar and Lounge
With a horseshoe shaped bar

(Courtesy of HCPL)

Hattie - Employee at the Paradise Bar

Ms. Hattie's sister was Sadye Gibbs Martin, the first woman Mayor of Plant City and the first African American woman elected mayor of a major city in Florida. Sadye Gibbs Martin served as mayor for seven terms and vice mayor for four.

Ms Hattie shared her sister's talent for management as she was in control of what happened at Paradise Bar.

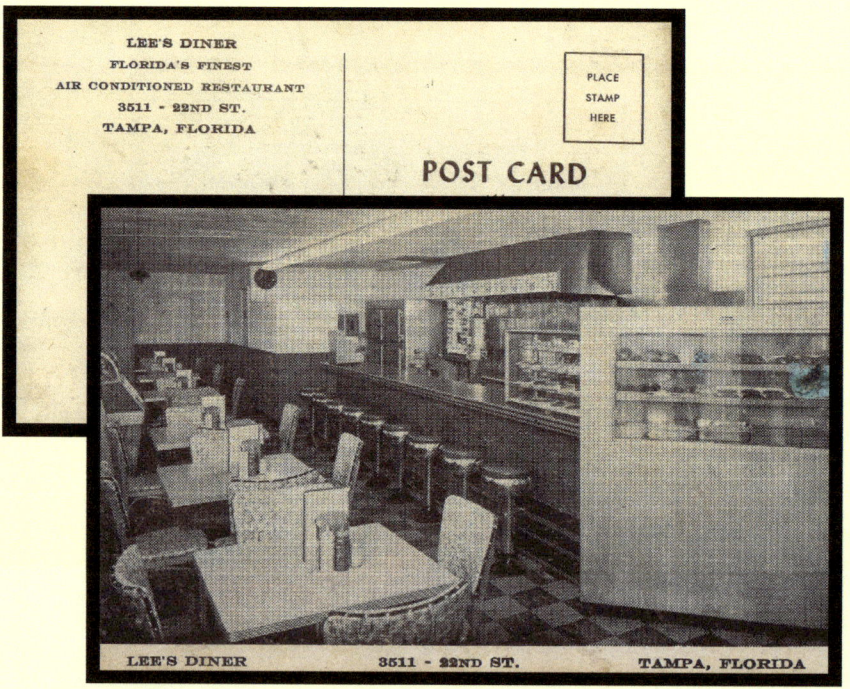

I used to help with some of the chores at Paradise. Even so, my father still made me pay for my meals.
He would say, "You eat it, you pay for it."

My Father - Lee Davis

Lee Davis and his friend, Ruye Hamilton, co-founded Washington Shores Federal Savings and Loan Association (later Metro Bank), the first black bank in Orlando, Florida in 1963. Lee Davis served as Vice-President. The bank was ultimately bought out by black billionaire, Bob Johnson. It now operates as Urban Trust Bank.

Lee Davis was chairman of Tampa chapter of National Negro Business League (NNBL) which was founded by Booker T. Washington in Boston, Massachusetts in 1900. The league strives to enhance the commercial and economic prosperity of the African American community. The NNBL was formally incorporated in 1901 in New York, and established hundreds of chapters across the United States. In 1966, the National Negro Business League was reincorporated in Washington, D.C. and renamed the National Business League. I remember some connection to a baseball team as a part of his association with the Business League, possibly the Negro Baseball League.

In the 1950s when my father would pick me up from school and take me with him to his Central Avenue businesses, seeing famous people and other dignitaries was a common occurrence. I got a chance to see countless stars just walking down the street or in the business establishments.

Around the time this photo was taken, I was placed on stage with my father's friend, Mary McLeod Bethune. She had just concluded a speech in Rogers Park and my task was to present her with flowers, which I did reluctantly. For doing so, Dr. Bethune rewarded me with a signed copy of one of her books.

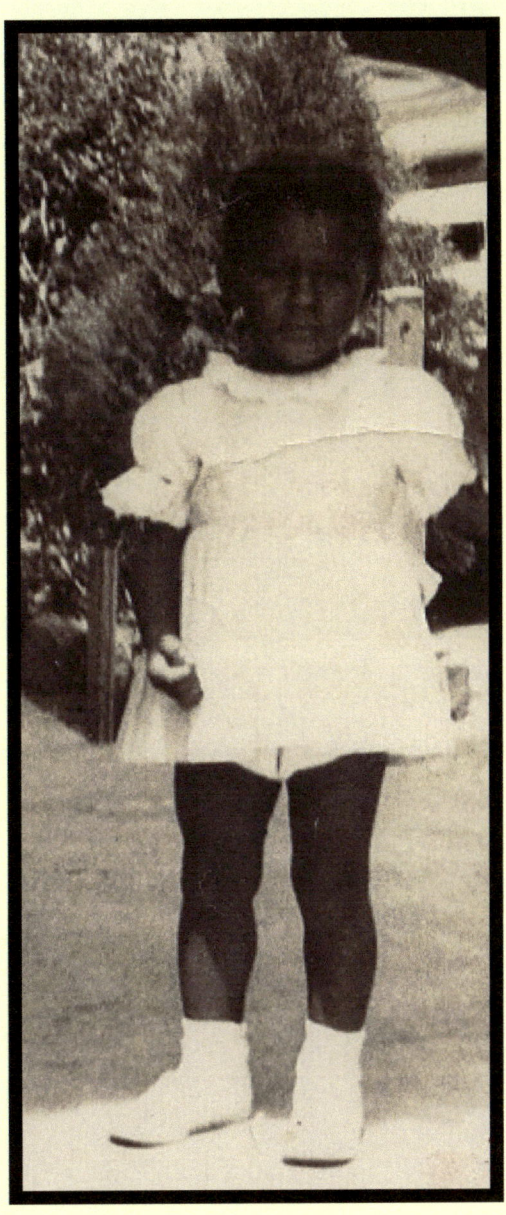

Bettye (age 5) on family vacation in Hot Springs, Arkansas, 1951

The Davis' home located at 3513 Potter Street. The house was built in 1936.

In the photo on the right, Davis was preparing to go hunting in the late 1940s.

My Father - Lee Davis

Davis pictured in his home next to a wall with his mounted fish and game.

Golfing with his friend at Roger's Park Golf Course.
Lee Davis, second from the right. Perry Harvey, Sr. is second from the left.

The Davis home at 3702 E Osborne Ave, which was built in 1960. Shown here is Dad's family from Georgia.

Ethel and Lee Davis (5th and 6th from left) at the popular Bellman and Waiter's Ball in the early 1960s

Lee Davis accepting an honorary Docorate degree from Dr. Richard Moore of Bethune Cookman College. The Davis' were staunch supporters of Dr. Bethune's College. (circa 1965)

Portrait of Lee Davis during dedication and placement in the Bethune Library.

Lee and Ethel Davis at Mary McLeod Bethune's home in Daytona Beach, Florida. Mr. & Mrs. Davis were friends of Mrs. Bethune's.

Lee Davis accepting an award

This Man's Best Friends

My father had 21 dogs at one time. He loved his dogs. The dogs had a man who would cook food just for them!

This was "Rock"

Part Five:
Remembering Mr. Davis

Carl Norton Remembers

Section 1 - THE PROLOG

Dr. Carl H. Norton, his daughter, Linda Norton circa 1950s, Tampa

The story starts around 1954, in Tampa, Florida. I was a 24-year-old young man, full of "vinegar" and excited about my life. I considered myself extremely fortunate to have been the son of Dr. Carl H. Norton, the most interesting person I had ever met in my 81 years of life. I am also proud to say that his associates felt the same way about him. It was no boring deal to get to know and interact with his associates. They were all interesting people. At the top of that list were Mr. Lee Davis, Tampa, Mr. Bill Small ("Pinch Penny"), the brother of Lee Davis' wife from the "Smalls" of Beaufort, S.C. and a descendent of the famous Robert Smalls (Probably one of the most interesting black men of the Civil War era and a personal friend of Abraham Lincoln, the former United States President. His history is worth researching. I recommend it.)

Also in my father's circle were Dr. Smith, Tampa, Dr. Cook, Virginia, Mr. William Clarence Smith, math teacher, Middleton H.S., John Henry Evans, teacher at Booker T. Washington School in Tampa, Rev. Floyd Johnson, Tampa. The list of associates would span distances from the complete East coast of the United States to Canada and then across the country to California where I had relatives, the Armwoods, who were doctors and research people. This introduction gives you somewhat of a brief idea of my family's friends and associates. (Esspecially my cousin Blanche Armwood, and I should include Mary McLeod Bethune, Daytona, and Mrs. Eleanor Roosevelt, President Franklin D. Roosevelt's wife.)

Carl H. Norton II, hunter and shooter, Tampa, Florida
(Photos courtesy of Carl N Norton II)

Now on to one singular adventure that included my family and their friend Lee Davis and others on a Thanksgiving Day turkey hunt.

Section 2 - THE HUNT

In late November just before Thanksgiving in 1954, I joined a turkey hunt with Mr. Lee Davis, John Henry Evans, Bill Small, Reverend Floyd Johnson, and my dad, Dr. Carl Norton. We were hunting on land owned by Lee Davis. It was a cattle ranch, a few hundred acres with a couple of hundred cattle, down near Ellington, south of Ruskin, Florida. The intent was to bag a few wild turkeys for Thanksgiving. I had never hunted turkey before, but I knew what they looked like. If I could get within range, I felt sure I could hit my target. Since I liked hunting alone and in quieter spaces, I settled on a large, beautiful wide open pasture, with a tall dead oak tree. I thought it would be a nice observation point. I sat under it and waited. In a short while, a large black bird soared directly at me not knowing I was there. He landed in the tree. My signature bark of the 20-gauge shotgun went "BANG!!!", and down fell the big black bird. One shot and I had my turkey!!

I picked up the bird and placed it in my shooting vest which had a large pocket for game in its rear holster. The bird filled the pocket. I put the vest back on and went to the car to show off my success. Bill Small said, "Carl, what is that I smell?" I said, "A turkey!" He said, "Let me see it." I pulled it out of the vest and his comment was, "a turkey all right...a turkey buzzard! Don't come near me please." I began to notice there was a horrible stink associated with my bird. We got a military shovel out of the trunk of my Father's car, and I proceeded to dig a hole and bury my bird along with my favorite hunting vest. It was a Red Head vest that was purchased from Sears & Roebuck in downtown Tampa. I hated to lose it, but I had no choice. It stunk! Driving home, I was forced to ride in the back seat of the car, with the windows down.

The hunting party was very amused at my trophy and for years called me "the Great Turkey Hunter" and then laughed out loud! Even though throughout my life, I hunted all across America and Europe, that month was the most memorable!

Good people!! THANK YOU, Mr. Lee Davis of Tampa, Florida, friend of my family!!

Dr. Charles Meyers Remembers

Charles Meyers was born and raised in Tampa, Florida, spent 12 years away in college, graduate school, dental school, the United States Army and returned to Florida in 1973. What follows are his memories of Lee Davis and his family.

My relationship, with Mr. Lee Davis began as a young man around nine years old when my family moved from the West Tampa Projects to the Belmont Heights Projects. Until then, Lee Davis was just a name I had heard. That's when I really came to know where he lived and what he looked like. In fact, my paternal grandmother lived diagonally across the street from his residence and some apartments that the owned. There was also a two-story apartment building directly behind their residence.

While in West Tampa, I had heard about Mr. Davis because he and another gentleman named Mr. Leon Claxton were very active in the community. Mr. Claxton, Mr. Davis, and a few others were people of financial means who were very generous. They were philanthropic, if you will, towards disadvantaged families, especially large families. For Christmas, they gave away bicycles, fire trucks, wagons, tricycles, and drums. They gave children major toys that were quality, genuine, American toys. My dad, Jason Meyers, often talked about what a big deal it was with young folk and what this gentlemen did. Mr. Claxton was the owner of the Harlem in Havana Show and traveled the country with the State Fair.

Dr. Charles Meyers (photo courtesy Dr. Meyers)

I never entered the Davis' home on Potter Street. However, my brother Jesse Meyers had a paper route distributing papers for Tampa Daily Times, and he was their paper boy. As such, he threw papers and at times went up to the door to collect money. Occasionly, I helped my brother and the times we approached the Davis' house, I saw that it was neat, clean, and just beautiful. They had a long driveway on Potter Street, a wall around the house, and big gated fence. Jesse was a couple of years older than me, graduated from Middleton High School, then from Florida A&M, and he had a year in as a medical student at Johns Hopkins when he had a fatal automobile crash in November 1971.

Mr. Davis' house was right across the street from some property that he donated for a health clinic. It was the precursor to the Hillsborough County Health Department's Lee Davis Clinic on North 22nd Street and 26th Avenue. The Potter Street clinic was the only clinic that was available to African Americans pre-integration. Later in 1966, during my senior year, the Davis family built a new home on Osborne Avenue.

In the Belmont Heights project, we were within walking distance from Mr. Davis' resident, and I got to know Mr. Lee and Mrs. Ethel beyond their legendary reputation. Mrs. Davis was a grand lady and a super person. My dad often spoke of her kindness and goodness.

I don't know what Mrs. Ethel Davis saw in me, but she treated me with the utmost respect, even though I had holes in my pants. She and Bettye took me on a tour of thier new home and it was amazing. That was the first time I saw a toilet that did not have the big tank in the back. They were expensive toilets with their baby's initials monogramed on them. I was in the house several times. Mrs. Davis even invited us over to talk about the fashion show, a community project of a social club I had joined, and offered to help us.

This was when I was a 10th grader at Middleton High School, and had joined the Ambassadors' Club. We were modeled after an actual fraternity, with our own emblem, high hat, and a cane. We wore red, white, and blue ribbons across our chest as to have the look of ambassadors when we had social events. I came to know Mr. Davis, the family man, due to Bettye Davis who happened to be his daughter.

It was during these planning sessions that I became aware of anyone using a checkbook and our club had one. We had a bank account, believe it or not, way back then in 1958. I later became president in 1960/61. At that time, Betty Davis was a freshman during Middleton's first year of having ninth grade. The Ambassadors' Club had an annual fashion show and we thought ourselves pretty fancy because our sponsor at the time was Dr. David Smith, a dentist who later became my dental office associate.

I mentioned Dr. Smith, because he and his wife, with their prominence and financials, were able to get into certain stores like MAAS Brothers and Belt Lindsay at a time when few others could. They purchased clothes for the young ladies to model in the fashion show. The show had about four scenes; a ballroom scene; a beach scene; a classroom scene and a "social somebody" scene. Bettye Davis was chosen as one of our models.

Well, with Mrs. Davis being the person she was, she made sure we had everything we needed. She was instrumental in making sure that some of the models got all of their clothes together. I don't think anybody had to spend one penny on anything due to Mr. and Mrs. Davis. That's when I became dear friends with Bettye Davis who was a kind, young lady. Therefore, I saw her father in action for myself. She was a kind, young lady who became a very dear friend.

From my point of view, he was one of the pioneers of this community because he was a "doer". Because of Mr. Davis one of my favorite lessons of the Bible is found in the book of Acts. The Acts of the Apostles. (1) The former treatise have I made, O Theophilus of all that Jesus began both to do and teach. (2) Until the day in which he was taken up. KJV I knew Mr. Davis as a person who was a "doer" first and then he would teach. He truly led by example.

I remember him also coming to the dental office and conversing with Dr. Smith (my partner in the dental office), more so than he did with me, but he was my patient for a while, believe it or not. I usually don't tell people who my patients are, but for this purpose I don't think he would mind. He was a very distinguished looking gentleman and a man of few words. His actions said it all. Once in December in the late 60s or 70s during a United Negro College Fund radio telethon, the funding was running low, Mr. Davis donated several thousands to make sure that our community/Tampa showed up well. He did these things, but you rarely heard him talk about it.

Mr. Davis had unfailing, unflinching support of Miss Ethel. She was behind him all the way in everything he did. And I remember Dr. Smith speaking of how they donated money when St. Paul's Church would have fundraising events. During one such fundraiser, the church was projecting they were short of their goal and Mr. Davis quietly stepped up and put forth the funding that they needed. Again, you didn't hear him. But you know, wherever he was, something was being done. Not saying that something would be done, it was being done.

When he did speak to you, he looked you straight in the eye. He wasn't a person who would look over you, even though his statue would permit it. He was at least six feet tall. He was a no-nonsense man who did not play. You knew he was about business. And you knew that he didn't have time to waste.

Over the years, my dad talked about him, and I saw him driving a hunting truck with cages for his trapping/hunting dogs. The truck came complete with a custom-built chair on it that was not "Jerry rigged". It was genuine, decent, store-bought stuff. Mr. Davis "did things" and that was the way he taught. He had hunting clothes too and he wore what reminds you of a British style hunting uniform, complete with boots that strung up to his knee. Regarding his attire, the great professor Dr. W. Mountain View Cobb at Howard University would have said that Mr. Davis was a sartorial splendor. Yes, he was a sartorial splendor as far as being neat, clean, and dressed for the occasion.

In my opinion, Mr. Davis didn't idolize people because I never of heard him just hanging around with certain celebrity-type people. In fact, Mr. Davis had friends in low places and all those, including me, had great respect for him. We honored him. I take it as a great privilege and an honor to be able to say, the little that I've been able to say.

Finally, Mr. Lee Davis was a remarkable businessman, loved his family and was good to his friends. They trusted him and he trusted them. Having known Mr. Davis, I attribute to my determination to give back to the community and to do for young folk. I've emulated him in some ways that led to young people coming up to me over the last few years and telling me about things that I did for them and their families. I did not have the money to do what Mr. Davis did, but I did what I could.

Part Six:
Our Family

Lee Davis Family Legacy

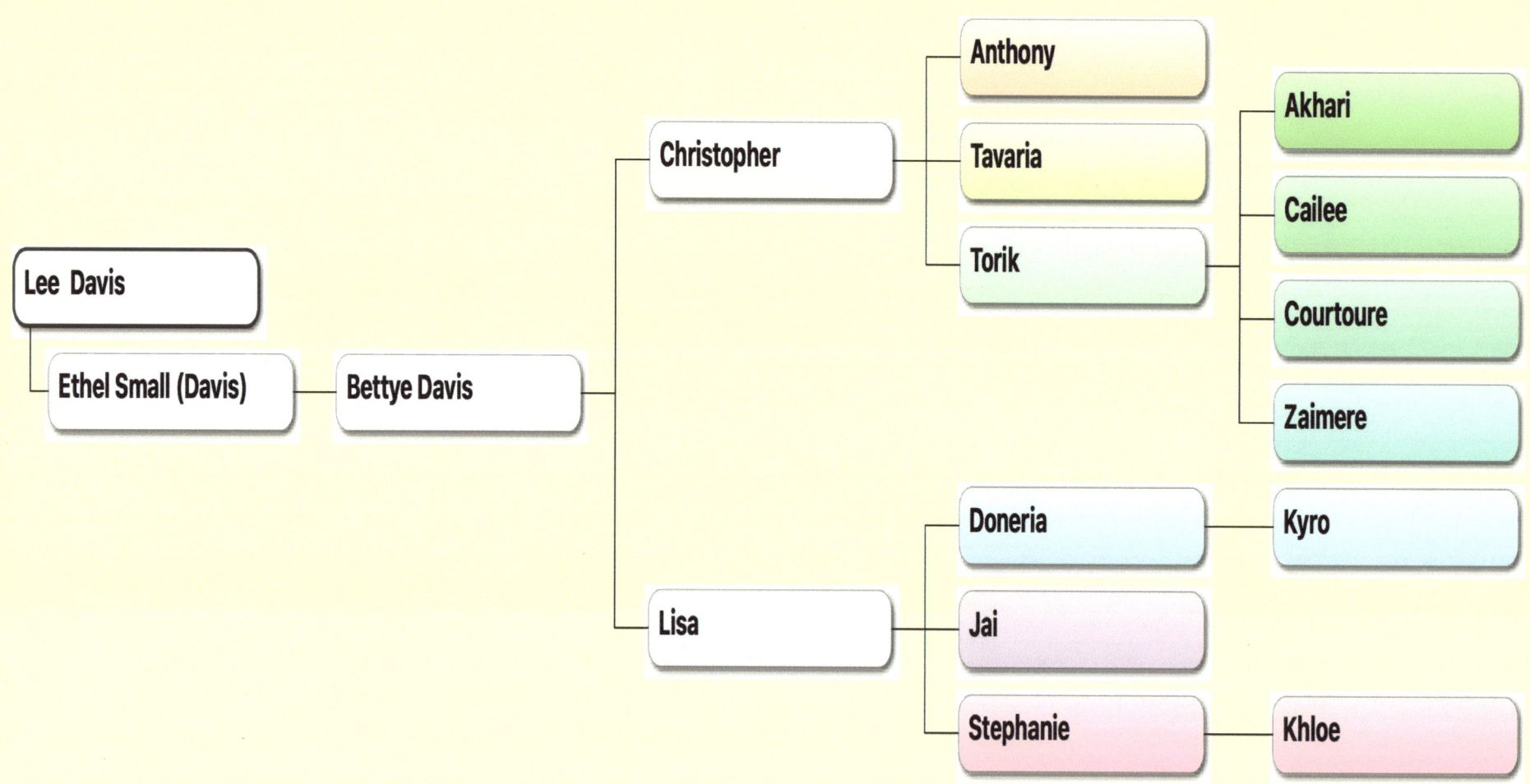

Ethel Davis (left), Lee Davis, Bettye Davis and Lillian B. Young at the Young's home on 21st Avenue in the early 1950s.

We were Ms. Young's guests for dinner.

Davis Family Legacy

My Father - Lee Davis

The Davis family is expansive and includes members of other well known families. However, their stories will remain their's to tell.

Given that Lee Davis met my mother in 1926 and they married on April 15, his birthday, they were indeed a gift to each other. The love they shared continues today, now including five generations. His legacy lives on.

Shown here is one of my dearest photos of my father and me. It was taken in 1951 while we were vacationing in Hot Springs, Arkansas. I was five years old. Over the years, my father took us on vacations every summer and upon our return, I had to write a paper detailing what I had learned.

The following are family photographs presented to comemorate our love and appreciation for a legend whose love travels in our hearts. The family is so proud to call Lee Davis our own.

Smalls Family Legacy

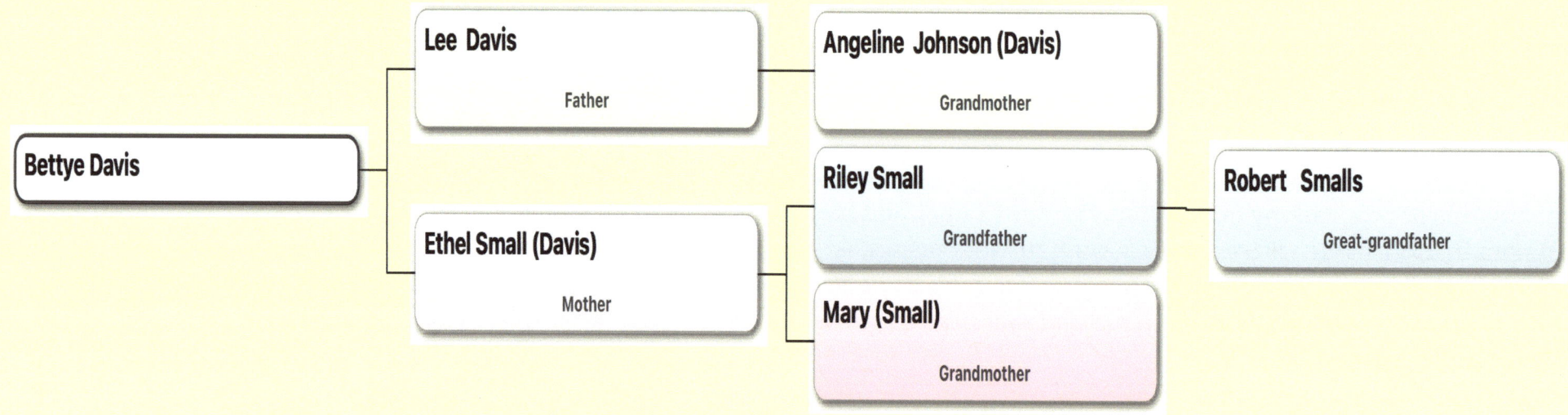

My Father - Lee Davis

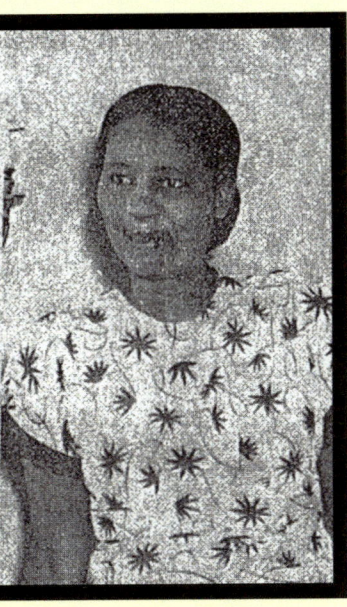

Robert Small* (April 5, 1839 – February 23, 1915)

Mary Small, Ethel Davis' mother, wife of Riley Small, Bettye's grandmother, Lee Davis' mother-in-law

Bill Small, Ethel Small Davis' brother, grandson of Robert Small circa 1940s Lee Davis' brother-in-law (Photo courtesy Carl N Norton II)

Mrs Ethel Small Davis, Lee Davis' wife and Bettye's mother, Robert Small's granddaughter

Robert Small was an American politician, publisher, businessman, and maritime pilot. Born into slavery in Beaufort, South Carolina, he freed himself, his crew, and their families during the American Civil War by commandeering a Confederate transport ship, CSS Planter, in Charleston harbor, on May 13, 1862, and sailing it from Confederate-controlled waters of the harbor to the U.S. blockade that surrounded it. He then piloted the ship to the Union-controlled enclave in Beaufort–Port Royal–Hilton Head area, where it became a Union warship. His example and persuasion helped convince President Abraham Lincoln to accept African-American soldiers into the Union Army. After the American Civil War he returned to Beaufort and became a politician, winning election as a Republican to the South Carolina Legislature and the United States House of Representatives during the Reconstruction era. Smalls authored state legislation providing for South Carolina to have the first free and compulsory public school system in the United States. He founded the Republican Party of South Carolina. Small was the last Republican to represent South Carolina's 5th congressional district until the election of Mick Mulvaney in 2011.

(Source: Wikipedia; Robert Smalls Photograph. https://www.loc.gov/item/2017893186/; *Small is spelling Bettye says is on family members' birth certificates)

Joe Lewis ate dinner at our home and was served from the china shown in this photo.

Father insisted that if you were at home, you were seated at the table and ate meals with the family. This included breakfast, lunch and dinner.

This is when adults discussed the events of the day and children shared what they learned.

Joe Louis, prizefighter wearing gloves. , ca. 1936. June 8. Photograph. https://www.loc.gov/item/2017657394/.

My Father - Lee Davis

Bettye Davis, daughter (Lisa), grandson (Torik) standing with Lee Davis artwork in the background - Perry Harvey, Sr. Park, Tampa FL

Bettye Davis, foreground; Lee Davis artwork, background - Perry Harvey Sr. Park, Tampa, FL

My daughter, Lisa

Workers at the Lee Davis Center. ukn, ukn, Mrs Hines (secretary) first from the left and Stephanie (manager of lee Davis Serivce Center), Mrs Margaret Jackson first from the right.

My granddaughter, Tavaria

My granddaughter, Stephanie

My Father - Lee Davis

Great grands Chloe & Kyro

Grandson, Torik

Grands
Torik & Doneria

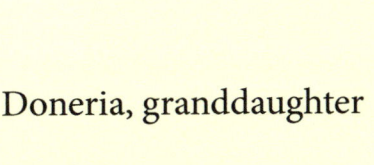

Doneria, granddaughter

Great grands Akhari, Cailee, Courtoure, & Zaimere

Great grands Zaimere & Akhari

Torik and his mother Natasha Mayes

Torik and his children

Great grandson Kyro

My Father - Lee Davis

Torik and his mother Natasha

I am shown here with Mrs. Rosa Parks in 1982 at the National NAACP in New York. I was there representing the Tampa Florida Branch as its president.

My Father - Lee Davis

Bettye Davis

Granddaughter Jai

Anthony

Part Seven
His Legacy:

"The Lee Davis Center"

Lee Davis Health Center's original location was at 28th and Potter Street.

The spirit of my father's legacy is also carried on in the work of Chloe Coney, founder The Corporation to Develop Communities (CDC) of Tampa, Inc., formerly known as Lee Davis Neighborhood Development Corporation, incorporated in 1992 for the purpose of alleviating poverty and physical deterioration in Hillsborough County's East Tampa Community. The CDC is not to be confused with Lee Davis Service Center on 22nd St.

Leader's Row

(Photos courtesy of E.K. Odom)

In 1979 the Perry Harvey Park was established by the City of Tampa under the leadership of Mayor William F. Poe; Lloyd Copeland-Chairman, Charles Miranda - Vice Chair, Catharine Barja, Lee Duncan, Sandra Warshaw Freedman, Jan Platt, and Charles Spicola, Jr.

The $6.3 million renovated park opened to the public on April 3, 2016 featuring the wonderful artwork as shown on the following pages from the Leader's Row section of the park.

Lee Davis is being honored by multiple points in the artwork at the Perry Harvey Park in Tampa, Florida. The artwork is the work of Michael Parker, an American artist born in 1977. The artistic process is called hand plasma cut aluminum, sandblasted and stained concrete.

"A Man with the power to take what he wanted but with the compassion to give all he had."

Artwork depicting Lee Davis and his work appears on Leaders' Row in Perry Harvey Sr. Park via a photo of him and his moble Heath Test truck.

(Photos: Courtesy of E.K. Odom)

The Davis Pool Room appears here in the 1100 block of Central Avenue as shown on Leader's Row.

The Pryamid Hotel appears here in the 1000 block of Central Avenue as shown on Leaders' Row.

Lingering memories of a great life style

This insert reveals that the magnificence of the Davis' home has survived decades. (Photo: Bettye Davis)

All too often, all memories of African American existence are abolished. No so in this case. In 1967, the Davis house was described by the Florida Accent as having a screened-in swimming pool, a circular driveway and a roofed drive-up entrance that usually had a new Cadillac in the driveway. The home was listed as having shrubbery as well as a brick and wrought-iron fence. The Davis' former home still exists in all its splendor, thanks to the subsequent owners. (Photo:Courtesy of E.K. Odom)

The poem, The Bridge Builder always reminds me of him saying how he always wanted to do things to help other people. How he wanted to leave something so that the world would know or the children who came behind him would know, that someone cared about them.

I like to remember my father as the bridge builder because that is what he wanted. The poem was his favorite and that is who he was.

He said it was his favorite poem because he wanted people to remember him as a bridge builder.

The Bridge Builder

Will Allen Dromgoole -Member of
St. Paul African Methodist Episcopal Church.

An old man, going a lone highway,
Came at the evening, cold and gray
To a chasm, vast and deep and wide,
Through which was flowing a sullen tide.
The old man crossed in the twilight dim,
That sullen stream had no fears for him;
But he turned when he reached the other side,
And built a bridge to span the tide.

"Old man," said a fellow pilgrim near,
"You are wasting your strength in building here.
Your journey will end with the ending day;
You never again will pass this way;
You've crossed the chasm deep and wide,
Why build this bridge at evening tide?"

The builder lifted his old gray head;
"Good friend, in the path I have come,"
he said, "There followed after me today
A youth whose feet must pass this way.
This chasm that has been as naught to me
To that fair-haired youth may a pitfall be;
He, too must cross in the twilight dim;
Good friend, I am building this bridge for him!"

www.ingramcontent.com/pod-product-compliance
Lightning Source LLC
Chambersburg PA
CBHW042107090526

44590CB00005B/133